WOODLAND BIRD SONGS & CALLS

Hannu Jännes
and Owen Roberts

WOODLAND BIRD SONGS & CALLS

Hannu Jännes
and Owen Roberts

NH
NEW
HOLLAND

First published in 2013 by New Holland Publishers
London • Cape Town • Sydney • Auckland
www.newhollandpublishers.com

Garfield House, 86–88 Edgware Road, London W2 2EA, UK
80 McKenzie Street, Cape Town 8001, South Africa
Unit 1, 66 Gibbes Street, Chatswood, New South Wales, Australia 2067
218 Lake Road, Northcote, Auckland, New Zealand

3 5 7 9 10 8 6 4 2

A CIP catalogue record for this book is available from the British Library.

ISBN 978 1 78009 248 5

Publisher and editor: Simon Papps
Design: Ann Pearlman
Production: Marion Storz
Printed and bound in China by Toppan Leefung Printing Ltd.

Other titles available in this series:
Bird Songs and Calls (ISBN 978 1 84773 779 3)
Common Garden Bird Calls (ISBN 978 1 84773 517 1)
Wetland Bird Songs and Calls (ISBN 978 1 78009 249 2)

CONTENTS

INSIDE BACK COVER
CD with bird sounds of 80 woodland species

INTRODUCTION TO WOODLAND BIRD SOUNDS

Ask Europe's top birders, especially those that earn their living as bird tour leaders, how many species they identify first by song or call and I think most people would be surprised by their answer. They would probably all say more than 50 per cent, but some, especially those who do much of their birding in closed environments such as forests, would perhaps go as high as 80 or even 90 per cent.

I have been fortunate enough to spend many hours in the company of some of our best field observers and, without exception, they hear and usually then identify a bird before they even raise their binoculars. It works both ways too, as if they don't immediately recognize the sound, then it is likely to be something unusual and therefore worth spending time on following up.

Of course, many years of experience, to say nothing of hard work, go into attaining such levels of expertise, but visits to your local forest or woodland soon after dawn in spring for the dawn chorus of singing birds should be an important first step. Male birds sing for two reasons – to proclaim their ownership of a territory in which to breed and to advertise their presence to females. Song is usually at its loudest and most protracted during the early stages of a male arriving on territory. Resident birds have foregone the

advantages conferred by migrating to warmer regions with more reliable food sources, to enable them to have the pick of the best territories early in the year. So it is our resident forest and woodland birds that start to sing first, with some, like the Song Thrush, in full song well before Christmas time. Those that have migrated return at intervals during April and May, with, in Britain at least, the Spotted Flycatcher last to arrive in mid- or even late May. So several visits to a site from late winter to late spring will enable you to pick up, and memorize, the songs and calls of each species as it arrives on breeding territory. If you are lucky enough to live close to a woodland nature reserve, you can speed up this process by attending one of the many dawn chorus events held by organisations such as the Wildlife Trusts, where experienced birders will be on hand to kick-start your skills.

By putting in a little time in these ways and using the images, text and particularly the CD of this book, even the novice birder should quickly gain confidence in putting names to the birds seen or heard in the forests and woodlands that, though sadly much diminished, still cover a substantial part of Britain and the rest of Europe.

OWEN ROBERTS

HOW TO USE THIS BOOK

- This book, together with the CD, teaches you to recognize some of the amazing sounds our birds make. The book features a photograph and some information on each of the 80 birds. It tells you where to find them, if they are here all year or only visiting us, what they eat and how they nest.

- Use the CD with the book to match the pictures of the birds with the sounds they make. The track numbers on the CD correspond with the numbering of the birds in the book.
- As you learn and remember the sounds, you will be able to look for those birds when you hear them. Simply follow the call and look for the bird that is making it.

CD track number and common name of bird.

Icons indicating food and nesting information.

Information about the call and the corresponding track number.

4 | Hazel Grouse
Bonasa bonasia

This small gamebird inhabits the dense, dark coniferous forests of northern and eastern Europe, and is more often heard than seen. However, when seen well, the male is a most handsome bird of intricately patterned browns and greys with a black chin, extensively bordered white, and a black, white-edged tail. The female is more brownish overall and lacks chin markings. Both have a discreet head crest, which is longer on the male. They often perch in the open on a tree branch and this provides the best chance of seeing one well. The Hazel Grouse is absent from Britain.

Berries and shoots; insects in summer.

Nest in dense ground cover where sitting bird becomes virtually invisible.

TRACK N° 04

Voice best clue to presence. First piping song of male, then series of calls by female, which takes off at the end of the sample.

5| Willow Grouse
Lagopus lagopus

While the British subspecies, the Red Grouse, is a bird of open heather moorland, the Willow Grouse is confined to the birch, conifer and willow forests found across much of the rest of northern Europe. Both sexes have almost all-white plumage in winter for camouflage, becoming reddish-brown on the head and neck in spring, with these areas extending and darkening as summer progresses. In May and June, the male sports bright red combs above the eyes. The wings remain white throughout the year.

Berries, young shoots and leaf buds, but young fed on insects.

Simple lined scrape in dense ground cover.

TRACK N° 05

Three samples of the advertising call issued by perched male.

11

1 | Goldeneye
Bucephala clangula

This diving duck is widespread in winter on lakes, reservoirs, large rivers and sheltered coasts, but in spring and summer it is found in forested areas close to water in northern Europe. The male is black and white with a glossy green head that has a large white spot behind the bill. The female is overall grey with a white collar and brown head. Both show conspicuous white wing-patches as they rise from the water in a rapid flurry of wings, which makes the whistling sound that has earned them their country names of 'Whistler' and 'Rattlewing'.

 Dives for molluscs, crustaceans and insect larvae.

 Tree holes and will use nest boxes.

2 | Goosander
Mergus merganser

The Goosander is a large 'saw-billed' diving duck, so called because its bill is serrated to hold slippery fish. The male is mainly white with a glossy greenish-black head, a red bill and black back. The female is grey with a brown head, which has a mane-shaped crest from nape down to neck, and a white chin and fore-neck. It winters and breeds in similar habitats to Goldeneye.

 Almost exclusively fish.

 As Goldeneye.

 TRACK N° 01

Peculiar whistling, sneezing and rasping noises, then musical whistling produced by wingbeats of a male.

 TRACK N° 02

First the display call of the male, then display call of a female with male audible in background.

3 | Capercaillie
Tetrao urogallus

The capercaillie is a huge, turkey-shaped gamebird. The male is as big as a large goose and is dark slate-blue, with brown on the mantle and wings, and a long tail that is cocked and fanned during display. The much smaller female is orange-brown with blackish barring and a large chestnut patch on the breast. It inhabits dense, especially mature, coniferous forests with a berry-bearing bush understory. In Britain, it became extinct in the 18th century, but it was reintroduced in the 19th century and is today scarce and confined to the forests of Speyside. It also occurs across northern Europe and in mountainous regions elsewhere in the continent as far south as Greece and Spain. Males gather at dawn leks where they display to females.

One male may mate with several females, but they play no part in incubation or rearing the young. Occasionally males, known as rogues, become aggressive and will even attack people who transgress into their territory.

 Food mainly pine needles (birds often swallow gravel at roadsides in order to digest these), but also berries and leaves.

 Nest is a scrape lined with leaves and mosses in dense ground cover.

TRACK N° 03

Lekking male's full popping and bubbling display calls, including two wing fluttering 'jump flights'.

4 | Hazel Grouse
Bonasa bonasia

This small gamebird inhabits the dense, dark coniferous forests of northern and eastern Europe, and is more often heard than seen. However, when seen well, the male is a most handsome bird of intricately patterned browns and greys with a black chin, extensively bordered white, and a black, white-edged tail. The female is more brownish overall and lacks chin markings. Both have a discreet head crest, which is longer on the male. They often perch in the open on a tree branch and this provides the best chance of seeing one well. The Hazel Grouse is absent from Britain.

 Berries and shoots; insects in summer.

 Nest in dense ground cover where sitting bird becomes virtually invisible.

5| Willow Grouse
Lagopus lagopus

While the British subspecies, the Red Grouse, is a bird of open heather moorland, the Willow Grouse is confined to the birch, conifer and willow forests found across much of the rest of northern Europe. Both sexes have almost all-white plumage in winter for camouflage, becoming reddish-brown on the head and neck in spring, with these areas extending and darkening as summer progresses. In May and June, the male sports bright red combs above the eyes. The wings remain white throughout the year.

 Berries, young shoots and leaf buds, but young fed on insects.

 Simple lined scrape in dense ground cover.

TRACK N° **04**

Voice best clue to presence. First piping song of male, then series of calls by female, which takes off at the end of the sample.

TRACK N° **05**

Three samples of the advertising call issued by perched male.

6 | Sparrowhawk
Accipiter nisus

This rather small bird of prey is found in most wooded parts of Britain. The species is resident in Britain, but highly migratory from north of its range.

The male, which is considerably smaller than the female, is blue-grey above and pale below, with some rufous on cheeks and breast. The female is grey-brown above, with a prominent white supercilium, and pale, heavily barred brown below. Immatures resemble the female but are streaked rather than barred on the underparts.

Sparrowhawks are slim-bodied with long tails and short broad wings, which make them supremely adapted to dashing through trees and bushes in pursuit of small birds. They typically fly with a series of shallow flaps followed by a glide.

Almost exclusively small birds. The species' excellent manoeuvrability allows it to move at speed through wooded areas to snatch birds such as tits and finches by surprise. Females can take larger prey up to the size of a Woodpigeon.

A substantial platform of twigs is erected in a broadleaved or coniferous tree, often based in the remains of an old crow's nest or squirrel's drey.

TRACK N° 06

Usually only vocal near nest. Quiet *kee-kee-kee* begging calls of fledged juveniles.

7 | Goshawk
Accipiter gentilis

A much larger version of the Sparrowhawk, the Goshawk is about the size of a Buzzard, or slightly larger. The female is larger than the male and both sexes have plumage similar to the female of their smaller cousin, with darker ear coverts and a much bolder white supercilium.

They are found in extensive mature coniferous forests, where the dashing hunting technique mimics that of the smaller species, but they also spend much time soaring above the forest, looking for prey below. They are easiest to see in spring, when the soaring, plunging display over the treetops is very spectacular.

 Rabbits, squirrels and birds up to the size of a Pheasant.

 A bulky tree nest.

8 | Common Buzzard
Buteo buteo

With a reduction in persecution, this medium-sized raptor is now a fairly common sight wherever there are trees in which to nest and roost with nearby open country to hunt. In Britain they are mainly dark brown with a pale crescent on the lower breast, but extremely variable elsewhere in Europe, with some very pale and others all dark. They are seen perched in roadside trees and on fence posts, but more often soaring over woodland with broad wings held in a shallow V-shape.

 Young rabbits and other small mammals, carrion and worms.

 Bulky, mainly in large trees, but also cliff ledges.

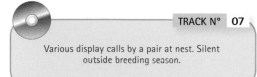

TRACK N° **07**

Various display calls by a pair at nest. Silent outside breeding season.

TRACK N° **08**

Vocal for a bird of prey, especially in flight when utters plaintive mewing calls. These are followed by a series of nasal calls.

9 | Green Sandpiper
Tringa ochropus

While this medium-sized wader is more usually seen in freshwater habitats on passage and in winter, it is a tree nester in the more waterlogged forests of northern Europe. Dark above with white spotting and white below, it is most often seen rising from the ground if flushed, when the back looks blackish in contrast to its prominent white rump and belly, giving it the look of an oversized House Martin. On the ground it habitually bobs its rear body. A very early return migrant, with adults seen in Britain as early as late June.

 Insects, molluscs, crustaceans and worms.

 Deserted squirrel drey or old thrush nest in trees.

10 | Woodcock
Scolopax rusticola

Similar in shape to a plump, outsized snipe, the Woodcock frequents deciduous and mixed woodlands with damp soil in which to feed by probing for insects with its long, stout bill. The sexes are similar and the plumage is an intricate mix of browns, buffs and blacks with dark bars across the head and neck.

Woodcocks are crepuscular and rarely seen during the day unless flushed, when they rise suddenly from the ground with a sound like cloth tearing. They are most often seen when the male performs its 'roding' display flight, quartering the forest at dawn and dusk on a regular route with fast, jerky wingbeats uttering a series of peculiar croaking and whistling sounds.

 Worms and insects.

 Simple depression in fallen leaves.

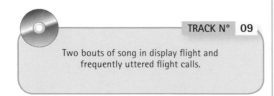

TRACK N° **09**

Two bouts of song in display flight and frequently uttered flight calls.

TRACK N° **10**

Roding display flight of the male. Not usually vocal outside breeding season.

11 | Stock Dove
Columba oenas

The Stock Dove is resident in places with mature trees including open woodland, parkland, larger town parks and even gardens throughout Britain, except for the west and north of Scotland. Birds that breed in north and eastern Europe are migratory and winter in southern and western Europe.

The species lacks the white on the wing and neck of the Woodpigeon and has a less powerful flight than that species. It is superficially similar to the ubiquitous Feral Pigeon of our towns and cities, being blue-grey with glossy green neck patches and a purplish tinge to the upper breast. In flight it has broad pale grey wing-panels and two small, black wing-bars are obvious, but these are not nearly so extensive as those on the commonest forms of Feral Pigeons. Stock Doves are often seen feeding in fields in the company of Woodpigeons and Feral Pigeons.

 Most vegetable matter including grain, weeds (especially charlock), young shoots and seedlings.

Usually in a hole in a mature tree, more occasionally in a building, rabbit burrow or ivy.

TRACK N° 11

Two samples of the low hooting song – *oo-wuh-ooo-wuh* repeated 8–9 times in a series.

12 | Woodpigeon
Columba palumbus

The Woodpigeon is common in woodlands and forests, and in any habitat where there are trees or large bushes in which to roost and nest, even in large towns and cities. This bulky grey pigeon is very like a larger, plumper version of a Stock Dove, but it is instantly recognisable by the prominent white markings on the wings and neck (although the white neck patch is absent in the juvenile).

A loud clatter of wings as it takes off draws attention to its presence. Woodpigeons are often seen in display flights, during which they climb rapidly to a height, clap their wings, then glide slowly downwards on stiff wings.

Woodpigeons are resident in Britain, although in winter the population is augmented with migrants that bred in northern and eastern Europe and retreat south and west. During this season the species can form vast flocks.

 Berries, cereals, seeds, weeds, which are supplemented by beechmast and acorns in autumn.

Builds a simple platform of twigs in a tree or bush that can be easily seen from below.

TRACK N° 12

Two series of the commonly heard song or advertising call – a deep five-syllable hooting with a very characteristic rhythm.

13 | Cuckoo
Cuculus canorus

The Cuckoo's distinctive eponymous voice and parasitic breeding habits have always fascinated humans. A summer visitor to much of Europe from tropical Africa, it is widely, if thinly, distributed in a variety of open habitats with trees and bushes, including woodland and forest.

   Males are plain grey above with white underparts finely barred with grey. Most females are similar, but a few are rusty-brown, heavily barred above and more closely resembling the juvenile. The eyes, legs and base of the bill are yellow. With its long pointed wings, often held drooped when perched, and long tail, it is often mistaken for a small raptor such as a Kestrel or Merlin in flight.

 Insects including especially hairy caterpillars that are shunned by other birds.

 Lays eggs in nest of other birds. The resultant hatchling ejects the eggs/young of the hosts and is raised by them. Over 100 species have been parasitized, but among the most common are Meadow Pipit, Reed Warbler and Dunnock.

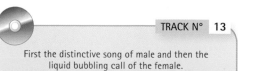

TRACK N° 13

First the distinctive song of male and then the liquid bubbling call of the female.

17

14 | Eagle Owl
Bubo bubo

Europe's largest owl has conspicuous ear-tufts and fierce orange eyes. Absent until recently from Britain, numbers of presumably escaped birds have begun a slow colonization. More typically it is a resident owl of forests and mountains in remoter parts of mainland Europe. The upperparts are blackish-brown mottled tawny-buff with barred wings and tail, the underparts paler and boldly streaked darker on the breast. It has huge talons.

 Smaller mammals, especially rats, and birds up to the size of ducks and gulls.

Sheltered ledges on cliffs and in ravines. More occasionally on the ground among boulders.

15 | Hawk Owl
Surnia ulula

This striking medium-sized owl has chiefly diurnal habits. It frequents more open areas of boreal forests, where it often sits on an exposed perch. It is more raptor-like in appearance than other owls, with a relatively slim body, long tail and short, pointed wings. It is brown with white mottling above and white with fine brown barring and streaking below. The black-bordered white facial disc is incomplete, with fierce staring yellow eyes. It will attack intruders, even people, when young are around the nest.

 Mainly voles and lemmings.

 In hollow trees or abandoned crow's nest.

TRACK N° 14

Barks of male, then male and female (female in the background) calling in duet, and finally calls of female with a distant male in the background.

TRACK N° 15

The bubbling song with a Long-eared Owl in the background.

16 | Pygmy Owl
Glaucidium passerinum

A tiny but entirely fearless owl, no bigger than a Starling, the Pygmy Owl is confined to the boreal forests of northern Europe and dense coniferous forests of central Europe. Grey-brown above with fine white spotting, its white breast and belly are streaked brown. The facial disc is less prominent than on other owls, but the yellow eyes still lend a fierce expression. It has a habit of waving its tail sideways. Active by day, it can be seen in bounding, woodpecker-like flight across open ground. In winter, it will leave the forest for more open areas with an abundant supply of its favourite prey – small birds.

 Mainly small birds and voles.

Holes in trees, especially those of woodpeckers. Also uses nestboxes.

17 | Tawny Owl
Strix aluco

The Tawny Owl is found throughout Europe, except Ireland and those regions above the treeline. It frequents areas of broadleaved or mixed woodland including parks, large gardens and tree-lined avenues in towns. In Britain it is usually tawny-brown with darker streaking and vermiculations, but a morph with a grey base colour is also widespread elsewhere in Europe. This is the owl that hoots. It has a close association with humans through the attraction our farms and other dwellings have for mice and rats.

 Mainly small rodents.

 In holes, usually in a tree, and will take readily to a nestbox.

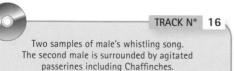

TRACK N° 16

Two samples of male's whistling song. The second male is surrounded by agitated passerines including Chaffinches.

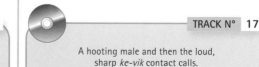

TRACK N° 17

A hooting male and then the loud, sharp *ke-vik* contact calls.

18 | Ural Owl
Strix uralensis

The Ural Owl occupies a similar range and habitats to the Great Grey, but with isolated populations in the higher mountain forests of south central Europe. It is another large grey owl, but it has a plain facial disc and is overall more buff-tinged and darkly streaked. Numbers do not fluctuate as much as other northern owls, presumably as they are able to take prey other than rodents. It is very aggressive at the nest, when it will even attack people without warning and with purpose!

 Staple is voles, but known to catch and eat small birds in poor rodent years.

 In a hollow tree stump, and will use nestboxes.

19 | Great Grey Owl
Strix nebulosa

This large owl is mainly confined to the great lowland boreal forests of northern and north-eastern Europe. Its plumage has much grey and white, but the facial disc is especially striking, with fine vermiculations around the eyes like the growth rings of a tree, white bows around the bill, a black chin and bright yellow, staring eyes. Its presence is dictated by the availability of voles, and a poor vole year can result in complete disappearance, even from previously favoured areas.

 Rodents, mainly voles.

 Large stick nest; often abandoned raptor's nest.

TRACK N° 18

First the typical, most often heard, three-note hooting of the male, then male and female duetting (female's call being the much coarser) and finally the commonly heard *hoohoooohoohoo* advertising call.

TRACK N° 19

First two series of deep powerful hoots by male, then another weaker type of hooting series, followed by a coarser series of hoots apparently produced by the female.

20 | Long-eared Owl
Asio otus

The Long-eared Owl is mainly nocturnal and well distributed throughout Europe in forests and woods with open country nearby over which to hunt. Its buff-brown upperparts are finely speckled darker, and its paler buff underparts are streaked brown with dusky bars forming arrow-shaped markings. The facial disc is pale rufous with prominent orange eyes. The ear tufts are obvious when raised, but in flight, and often at rest, they are lowered. It roosts communally in winter with sometimes dozens of birds occurring in a single tree, especially in central Europe.

 Voles and small birds.

In trees in an old crow nest, especially those of Magpie.

21 | Tengmalm's Owl
Aegolius funereus

This small owl has a disproportionately large head. Strictly nocturnal and very difficult to see away from the nest, it inhabits dense forests in northern and central Europe. Its dark brown back is mottled white, with the white underparts heavily streaked and barred brown. The facial disc is greyish-white with prominent eyebrows that give it a perpetually surprised look. Heavily dependent upon voles, it can disappear almost completely from even favoured areas in poor rodent years.

 Almost exclusively voles.

Holes in trees, especially old Black Woodpecker holes. Will use nestboxes where provided.

TRACK N° 20

First male's rather weak series of single hoot notes, then powerful wing-claps and hoot notes in display flight. Finally 'squeaky gate' begging calls of fledglings.

TRACK N° 21

Two samples of the song, the first delivered at normal speed, the second by an excited male in the presence of a female. Finally nasal calls of a female.

22 | Nightjar
Caprimulgus europaeus

The nightjar is a nocturnal bird with a huge gape for 'netting' insects in flight in the woodland clearings and rides where it is found. Often its distinctive 'churring' song at dusk is the first indication of its presence.

The Nightjar is not much larger than a Blackbird, but it has much longer wings and tail. Its grey-brown base colour is heavily streaked and vermiculated with black, pale rufous and cream. The species is most often seen if flushed from its roost (which is usually lengthwise along a thick tree branch) or when hawking insects in the half-light. In flight, the white patches on the outer wings and tail tips of the male are prominent, although these are lacking in the female.

Nightjars breed in suitable habitat throughout Europe, except for the far north. In Britain it is rather localized and it is scarce in Scotland and Ireland. The birds are generally present at the breeding grounds from May to September, and they spend the winter in Africa.

 Insects, especially moths, taken on the wing.

 On bare ground in open woodland or on dry heath with trees and scrub.

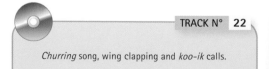

TRACK N° 22

Churring song, wing clapping and *koo-ik* calls.

23 | Lesser Spotted Woodpecker
Dendrocopos minor

This tiny woodpecker is not much bigger in size than a sparrow – it is often difficult to appreciate how small it actually is until seen. The Lesser Spotted is the only black-and-white European woodpecker to lack red or pink on the undertail-coverts. The upperparts are black with bold white barring and the underparts are white with narrow streaking. The female's crown is black and the male's is red. The bill is noticeably smaller than in other woodpeckers. Its flight is strongly undulating, like most of the other woodpecker species.

The species is widely distributed across Europe, but it is rather localized in England and not found at all in Scotland or Ireland. It frequents all types of deciduous woodland including orchards, parks and even large gardens, and is often found with roving tit flocks in autumn and winter. Drum is high-pitched and very rapid.

 Predominantly small arboreal insects.

 Excavates hole in a dead tree.

TRACK N° 23

Characteristic rapid drumming, then a sample that includes the fast series of piping advertising calls, and short chick calls that are similar to those of Great Spotted.

24 | Middle Spotted Woodpecker
Dendrocopos medius

This pied woodpecker is commonest in the mixed deciduous woods of central Europe. Through most of its range, large, mature oaks seem essential. It has never been recorded in Britain. The Middle Spotted is similar to the Great Spotted, but it is slightly smaller, has pinkish tinged underparts and pale red rather than crimson undertail-coverts. It has less black on the face than other pied woodpeckers, the head being almost entirely white with a red crown. It has a fairly weak bill for a woodpecker and rarely drums.

 Arboreal insects from surface of wood.

 Excavates hole in rotten trunk or branch.

25 | White-backed Woodpecker
Dendrocopos leucotos

Almost entirely absent from Western Europe, it is a bird of the wet mixed forests of central and eastern parts of the continent. It is by far Europe's rarest woodpecker, because modern forestry methods clear the areas of the dead and dying trees that it requires. The white back shows most clearly in flight: at rest, it is often covered by the barred black-and-white wings. The underparts are pale buff with black streaking, and the undertail and crown are pale red.

 Wood-boring and bark-living insects extracted from rotten wood.

 Excavates a hole in a tree.

TRACK N° **24**

Series of nasal calls.

TRACK N° **25**

First drumming by a pair, then typical kick calls and some tapping, and finally excited calls by two birds.

26 | Great Spotted Woodpecker
Dendrocopos major

By far the commonest of Europe's pied woodpeckers, the Great Spotted is found everywhere with woodland habitat, including parks and large gardens even in semi-urban environments. It is black above with large oval 'shoulder' patches, while the underparts are white with a prominent crimson patch under the tail. Both sexes have white cheeks with a black stripe running from the bill to the nape, and a black crown, with a small crimson patch on the nape of the male. Confusingly, the juvenile has an entirely red crown.

The Great Spotted drums more than any other European woodpecker species and can do so at any time of the year, although the peak period is when the birds are proclaiming their territories in early spring. In Britain the species is a regular visitor to bird tables. It is common across England, Wales and Scotland, and the population has been increasing in recent years, but it is absent from Ireland.

 Insects, seeds and the eggs and nestlings of other birds.

 Excavates a hole in a tree.

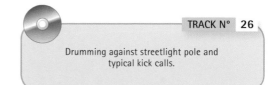

TRACK N° 26

Drumming against streetlight pole and typical kick calls.

27 | Three-toed Woodpecker
Picoides tridactylus

As the name suggests, this is the only European woodpecker with three, rather than four, toes on each foot. The plumage is strikingly black and white, relieved only by the yellow on the crown of the male. Extremely arboreal in its habits, it is found in mature conifer and mixed forests, particularly in Europe's taiga belt. It has never been recorded in Britain. Both sexes have loud, rattling drums, but when not drumming it is unobtrusive and very difficult to see.

 Insects, especially the larvae and pupae of the spruce bark-beetle.

 Excavates hole in a dead tree or stump.

28 | Black Woodpecker
Dryocopus martius

A very large crow-sized woodpecker. Widely distributed throughout most of Europe where mature forests exist, but never recorded in Britain. Glossy black with a bright red crown on the male, which is restricted to the hind crown on the otherwise similar female. A white eye and ivory base to the massive bill are very conspicuous. Unlike other woodpeckers flight is not bounding, but straight until it dips and swoops up just prior to landing. The drum-roll is exceptionally loud and far-carrying and has even been likened to machine-gun fire!

 Tree-dwelling insects, especially ants.

 Excavates nest hole in large tree often at the edge of clear-fell areas.

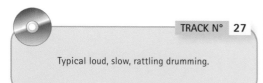
TRACK N° **27**

Typical loud, slow, rattling drumming.

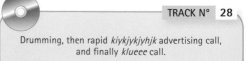
TRACK N° **28**

Drumming, then rapid *kiykjykjyhjk* advertising call, and finally *klueee* call.

29 | Green Woodpecker
Picus viridis

Green Woodpecker is a fairly common species in most of western and central Europe, including Britain, although it is not found in Ireland. It inhabits deciduous and mixed woodland, and is also found in well-wooded parks and even large gardens.

A large woodpecker, it is mossy-green above with a bright yellow rump that is conspicuous in flight (and can sometimes lead to it being mistaken for a Golden Oriole – see page 28), pale greenish below and has a bright crimson crown and a black mask around the eye. The sexes are superficially similar except that the male has a black-bordered crimson moustachial patch, which is all black on the female. The juvenile is greenish, and heavily barred and spotted all over.

The Green Woodpecker very rarely drums, but it does have a distinctive loud, laughing call often described as a 'yaffle'. Unlike most woodpeckers, it spends much of its time feeding on ground-dwelling ants.

 Diet consists almost entirely of ants.

Excavates hole in a large, mature deciduous tree, almost always on the main trunk.

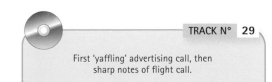

TRACK N° 29

First 'yaffling' advertising call, then sharp notes of flight call.

30 | Grey-headed Woodpecker
Picus canus

Similar to the Green Woodpecker, but the Grey-headed is slightly smaller and with greyer underparts and head, on which only the male has a crimson patch and that is restricted to the fore-crown. It is a bird of central Europe, where it occupies a wide range of habitats that provide large deciduous trees in which to nest and a plentiful supply of ants for food. It drums more frequently than the Green, sometimes using man-made sites such as telegraph poles and even tin roofs.

 Ground-dwelling ants, but also a wide range of other invertebrates.

 Excavates hole in deciduous trees that are rotten and easy to bore into.

31 | Golden Oriole
Oriolus oriolus

The thrush-sized male is a vivid yellow, with black wings and tail, and a bright red bill. The female is more subdued, with a greenish back and whitish underparts with narrow dark streaking. Despite being Blackbird-sized, and the male's bright colours, orioles are very difficult to see in their woodland habitat and are usually only glimpsed as they dash through more open areas. The species winters in Africa and is a summer visitor to the deciduous woodlands of Europe, although it is a very scarce bird in Britain.

 Insects, berries and fruit.

 A hammock suspended in a tree fork.

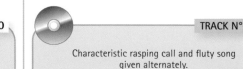

TRACK N° **30**

Drumming, advertising call, which is a slower version of the Green Woodpecker's 'yaffle', and other calls.

TRACK N° **31**

Characteristic rasping call and fluty song given alternately.

32 | Siberian Jay
Perisorcus infaustus

The Siberian Jay is confined to the dense coniferous forests of northernmost Europe, where it is resident. It is a small crow, not much bigger than a large thrush. Its plumage is mostly grey-brown with rust-coloured lower belly, rump, outer-tail and wing patches and a dark crown. It has a deeply undulating flight. Although normally of a retiring nature, the species is highly inquisitive and often investigates the presence of people briefly before disappearing into the forest again.

 Insects, small mammals, eggs and young of other birds, berries and seeds.

 A well-lined cup on a loose platform of twigs close to a conifer trunk.

33 | Jay
Garrulus glandarius

Europe's most colourful crow is found just about everywhere with tree cover, except for the far north. It is mainly resident but with some southward movement of northerly breeders. It is overall a pinkish grey-brown with a black moustache and white vent. It is particularly striking in flight, when the white and pale blue wing patches and the white rump are shown to best effect. Common, but very shy and seldom seen well, its presence is often only betrayed by its harsh, screeching alarm call.

 Larger insects, eggs and young of other birds, fruits and especially acorns that are gathered and stored in autumn for winter.

 Well concealed in a small tree or bush.

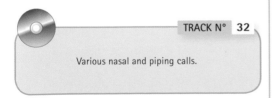

TRACK N° **32**

Various nasal and piping calls.

TRACK N° **33**

Various vocalizations of this noisy crow, including a perfect imitation of a Goshawk (third sample) and finally the most characteristic raucous, hoarse screech.

34 | Nutcracker
Nucifraga caryocatactes

The nutcracker is found in the spruce zone of central and northern Europe, with some movement south in winter. It is most often seen perched at the very top of a spruce tree. The species is a very rare vagrant to Britain. About the size of a Jackdaw, it is dark brown and heavily spotted with white, with darker blackish wings and crown and a white tail tip and undertail-coverts. The dagger-shaped bill is huge and powerful looking.

 Conifer seeds, eggs and young of other birds, insects and nuts.

 Compact well-made structure next to trunk of a conifer.

35 | Woodlark
Lullula arborea

Europe's only woodland lark is found in areas of clear-fell and glades in forests, woods and on heaths with scattered trees and bushes. Unobtrusive on the ground, in the air it is more obvious, with a very short tail, broad wings and an undulating flight with rapid flaps interspersed with closed-winged glides. The upperparts are brown with dark streaking, the breast streaked brownish and the belly white. The head is well marked with chestnut cheeks bordered white and with the bold supercilia meeting at the nape. In Britain the species is confined mainly to southern England and East Anglia.

 Insects and seeds.

 A well-concealed lined scrape on the ground.

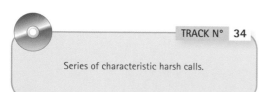

TRACK N° **34**

Series of characteristic harsh calls.

TRACK N° **35**

Examples of the beautiful whistling song.

36 | Marsh Tit
Poecile palustris

Widely distributed in Europe, including Britain, the Marsh Tit is not usually found in marshes as the name suggests, but most frequently in deciduous and mixed woodland, parks and large gardens. It is grey-brown above and off-white below, with white cheeks and a glossy black cap and bib. It joins mixed feeding flocks of tits and other small birds in winter, but only rarely strays far from its home territory.

 Mainly insects and seeds.

 Nests in a hole in a rotten tree trunk or slump, which it lines with wool, hair and moss. Also uses nestboxes.

37 | Willow Tit
Poecile montanus

Very like the Marsh Tit, the Willow Tit has a more bull-necked appearance and a pale panel in the closed wing. There are other small differences, such as the size of the bib, but these are difficult to discern in the field. The best clue to its identity is the nasal call, which is very different to that of the Marsh Tit. Its range and habitat overlap with the Marsh Tit, but with a preference for damp birch and alder woodland and conifers, so distribution reaches further north, where the birds are both larger and paler than those to the south.

 Insects and seeds.

 Excavates own hole, which Marsh Tit does not, in rotten tree or stump.

TRACK N° 36
Song a series of *twetwetwe* repeated every three seconds. Characteristic calls include a sharp *ssi* or *pssi* chew, often with a scolding nasal *jhe jhe jhe jhe*.

TRACK N° 37
Tiu tiu tiu song and two versions of characteristic nasal *tee tee dah dah* call.

31

38 | Siberian Tit
Poecile cinctus

The Siberian Tit is mainly resident in the lichen-festooned forests of the far northern parts of Europe, with some southward movement in winter. It has a brown back and off-white underparts with rust-coloured flanks. The head is disproportionately large, with white cheeks, and the crown is brown, rather than black as in other related species. The black bib extends to the upper breast as speckling.

Insects and seeds.

Hole in a conifer, birch or decaying stump. Will use nestboxes.

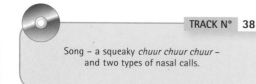

TRACK N° **38**

Song – a squeaky *chuur chuur chuur* – and two types of nasal calls.

39 | Coal Tit
Periparus ater

The size of a Blue Tit, the Coal Tit has a grey back and dusky-buff underparts. The head is black, with white on the cheeks and nape, and it has two prominent white bars on the wing. The sexes are similar. Mainly resident throughout much of Europe except the far north, it has a preference for coniferous woods, although it also inhabits deciduous woods and parks and gardens with some conifer element. It is common in much of Britain.

Insects and oil-rich seeds, especially those of spruce cones, and fat.

Holes in trees, but sometimes on, or close to, ground in tree roots or stumps.

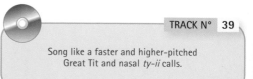

TRACK N° **39**

Song like a faster and higher-pitched Great Tit and nasal *ty-ii* calls.

40 | Crested Tit
Lophophanes cristatus

A common resident of coniferous forests over much of Europe, in Britain it is confined to the Caledonian pine forests of the Scottish Highlands. A small, very cute-looking tit with a greyish-brown back and whitish underparts, it is the black-and-white head pattern, complete with black-and-white crest, that give it such a distinctive, attractive appearance. It joins wandering flocks of other tit species in winter, but is only rarely seen away from extensively forested areas.

 Insects, spruce and pine seeds. Occasionally visits bird tables in the forest.

 Excavates hole in rotten tree.

41 | Great Tit
Parus major

The Great Tit is resident throughout Europe, where it is commonly found in all types of woodland, parks and gardens. The male is colourful, with a greenish back, bright yellow underparts, a black central stripe along the belly and a black head with white cheeks. The female is similar, but her colours are more subdued. It has a bewildering variety of calls, to the extent that unrecognized calls often prove to emanate from a Great Tit when the bird is seen.

 Insects, oil-rich seeds, berries and fat. A regular visitor to garden bird feeders.

 In a tree hole or nestbox, more occasionally in a wall.

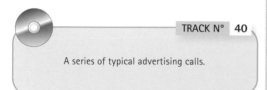

TRACK N° 40

A series of typical advertising calls.

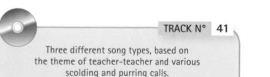

TRACK N° 41

Three different song types, based on the theme of teacher-teacher and various scolding and purring calls.

42 | Blue Tit
Cyanistes caeruleus

One of the most familiar birds in Europe, the Blue Tit's body plumage is superficially similar to that of the larger Great Tit, but it has more brightly coloured blue wings. Its head pattern is very distinctive – a mainly white face with a black eye-stripe, bib and collar, and a bright blue crown surrounded by a narrow border of white. Males and females are quite similar, but the males are slightly more brightly coloured. In juveniles the white areas on the head are replaced by pale yellow and the crown is greenish.

The Blue Tit is found throughout Europe, and is only absent from the extreme north. It is mainly resident, breeding in woodlands and especially in parks and gardens where it is a frequent visitor to bird tables and to nestboxes. In winter it often forages in reedbeds.

 Feeds on insects, seeds and soft fruit. Frequent at bird feeders and bird tables, where peanuts and fat are favourite constituents of its diet.

Nests in a hole in a tree or stump, or occasionally in a stone wall. Will readily use nestboxes.

TRACK N° 42

First the songs, including the short *tsee-tzi-tzii* and the beautiful high-pitched silvery *biibi-sisisisi-srrrrrrrrr*. Then two samples of calls including *churr* notes.

43 | Long-tailed Tit
Aegithalos caudatus

This cute-looking bird has a tiny bill, small body and very long, narrow tail. Its body length is 13–15cm, of which 7–9cm is the tail. Its plumage appears fluffy and is mostly black and off-white, with pinkish patches on the wings, rump and belly.

Around 20 subspecies of Long-tailed Tit have been recognized. The western European subspecies *rosaceus* has dark crown stripes and is common in Britain. The northern Eurasian subspecies *caudatus*, which is found from Scandinavia eastwards, is highly distinctive due to its completely white head.

The Long-tailed Tit is mainly resident in deciduous and mixed woods, parks and gardens throughout Europe, except in the extreme north. Families form into flocks that are restless and always on the move, while constant calling keeps members of the flock in contact.

Mainly small insects and spiders; will take seeds and fat at bird tables.

An amazing camouflaged ball of moss and lichens in a tree fork or bush with a very small entrance hole.

TRACK N° 43

First a series of slurred *trrrrr* calls and some little *ptt* notes interspersed with one strophe of the high-pitched, clear trilling song. Then shorter slurred *trr* calls and very high-pitched *titititi* calls.

35

44 | Nuthatch
Sitta europaea

This familiar woodland species is found in most of Europe. In Britain it is common in England, but rare in Scotland. It is absent from Ireland and northern Scandinavia.

Nuthatches are blue-grey on the back and crown, with white cheeks and a black stripe running from the bill through the eye to the shoulder. In most parts of Europe, including Britain, the underparts are rusty-orange, but in northern Europe, the birds have mostly white underparts, with any rusty colouration confined to the undertail-coverts.

The species has a disproportionately large bill and feet, which are put to use in running up, down and along tree trunks and branches looking for food. It is a highly vocal species, with a wide variety of advertising and territorial calls.

In summer, mainly invertebrates such as spiders and insects, including beetles and grubs. Larger seeds and nuts form a greater part of the diet in autumn and winter, when it often visits bird tables.

Nests in a tree hole. Often, if the hole is too large, the birds will plaster the entrance with mud to achieve the right dimensions.

TRACK N° 44

Two different song types, a rapid liquid trilling, *ve've've've've*, then a slow disyllabic *wee-wee* repeated every few seconds or so. Calls include an often-repeated *tuiep*.

45 | Treecreeper
Certhia familiaris

The Treecreeper's appearance and habits mean that it is like no other British breeding bird. Its brown upperparts are heavily marked with buff and black, while the underparts are plain whitish and the narrow bill is fairly long and slightly decurved, making it the ideal tool for probing wood for insects. The stiff tail is used to press against tree trunks to facilitate climbing, giving the bird the appearance of a tiny woodpecker.

This bird does exactly as its name suggests, creeping mouse-like up and along tree trunks and branches, but then flies down again, as, unlike the Nuthatch, it cannot descend a tree in this manner. It is resident in woods and parks across most of Europe, including Britain. In winter it often joins roaming tit flocks.

 Almost exclusively insectivorous, but also occasionally eats seeds.

 Nest is built on a supporting platform of small twigs behind the loose bark of a tree or in ivy. Will also use specially designed nestboxes.

TRACK N° 45

A quiet but distinctive *swee-swee-swee* song followed by a trill, high-pitched slightly trilling *tsirrr* and very high-pitched *tse*.

46 | Wren
Troglodytes troglodytes

Found throughout Britain and most of continental Europe, the diminutive Wren is one of our most familiar birds. It is resident in Britain, and populations can suffer badly during harsh winters. Populations that breed in Scandinavia migrate south for the winter.

The species is usually recognized by its small size, short tail, which is usually cocked, and very loud song for such a small bird. It is rusty-brown above, greyish-brown below, with some darker barring on the flanks, and has an obvious pale supercilium. Males, females and juveniles all look superficially similar.

Wrens are common in woodland and forest, as well as gardens, parks, and in fact anywhere where there are patches of dense cover in which to nest and feed. They are normally very territorial, and in winter they often roost communally with up to 20 birds crammed together in a suitable cavity.

 Small insects and spiders, more occasionally seeds.

 A dome built of grass, moss, lichen and leaves in a hedge, crevice or ivy.

TRACK N° **46**

An amazingly loud song with trills, then rattling, hard *zerrrrr* calls and sharp, clicking call notes.

47 | Goldcrest
Regulus regulus

Europe's smallest bird, the Goldcrest has a tiny bill and short tail. It is resident throughout much of its range, but for those breeding in northern and eastern Europe there is some movement south and west in autumn to milder regions, including Britain.

The Goldcrest is a conifer specialist in summer, when it has a preference for yews and cypresses, but at other times of year it is found in mixed woodlands, parks and gardens, and can often be seen accompanying tit flocks.

In all plumages, birds are pale green above and off-white below. The male has a bright orange crown-stripe, while this is plain yellow on the female. In both sexes the crown-strip has a broad black border, while the wing has two pale bars and a black band. The species is often best located by its high-pitched, constantly uttered, *zee-zee* call.

 Small insects such as aphids, often found on the undersides of leaves.

 A hammock of moss and lichens suspended from the branch of a conifer.

TRACK N° 47

Remarkably high-pitched rhythmic song, *treddle-e-dee*, repeated rapidly and often and ending in a flourish. Then equally high-pitched *zee-zee*, *zee-zee* calls.

48 | Willow Warbler
Phylloscopus trochilus

The Willow Warbler is one of a group of birds known as leaf warblers, which are frequently a source of confusion even to experienced birdwatchers, as they all have similar plumage. It is best distinguished from the very similar Chiffchaff by its song and call.

Typically this species is greyish-green above, pale yellowish on the breast and white on the belly, with a pale supercilium and brownish legs. Juveniles have brighter yellow underparts. Northern populations are greyer above and whiter below.

This is a very common breeding bird that is found in all types of woodland and scrub throughout northern and central Europe. It is a summer visitor from sub-Saharan Africa and is generally one of the first returning migrants each spring, with the first birds reaching southern England in late March.

 Almost exclusively insects, especially aphids and small caterpillars gleaned from leaves.

 A dome constructed of grass on or near the ground and concealed in thin vegetation.

TRACK N° **48**

The liquid, cascading song, followed by the *hyy-it* call, which is very similar to the call of the Chiffchaff, but slightly more upslurred at the end.

49 | Chiffchaff
Phylloscopus collybita

This bird is very similar in appearance to the Willow Warbler, but it tends to be a bit smaller and generally more drab above and dirtier white below, with little or no yellow on the breast. The supercilium is less well marked and it has darker legs. The song, a simple repetition of its name, is frequently heard and the best clue to its identity.

The Chiffchaff breeds across northern and central Europe in many habitats where there are tall deciduous trees with some undergrowth. It is a short-distance migrant, with most of the population spending the winter in Iberia or North Africa. The species was traditionally considered to be a summer visitor to Britain. This is still its primary status, but in recent years increasing numbers have been spending the winter in this country.

Invertebrates such as aphids, small larvae and spiders, which are often picked from leaves. Chiffchaffs often sally from trees to catch flying insects.

Domed grass nest close to, or on, ground in undergrowth such as brambles or small bushes.

TRACK N° 49

The repetitive *chiff-chaff, chiff-chaff* song, followed by the *hyit* call, which is less drawn out and more monosyllabic than the call of the Willow Warbler.

50 | Wood Warbler
Phylloscopus sibilatrix

Slightly bigger than the Willow Warbler, the Wood Warbler is brighter in all respects, with moss-green upperparts, yellow face and breast, very white belly and yellowish supercilium. A summer visitor from tropical Africa, the Wood Warbler is found in Britain between April and August and its breeding habitat is tall deciduous or mixed woodland with sparse undergrowth. It often stays high in the branches and is most easily detected by its song in spring.

 Arboreal insects and other invertebrates, and some fruits.

 A dome built of grass on the ground and well hidden in vegetation.

51 | Greenish Warbler
Phylloscopus trochiloides

Smaller than Willow Warbler and somewhat similar in plumage, but with colder, greyer tones. Best distinguished by the long whitish supercilium and the presence of a short whitish wing-bar. In Europe confined as a breeder to European Russia and the Baltic States, spending the winter in the Indian Subcontinent. It occurs in spruce or mixed forest, spending much of its time in the high canopy. A rare but increasing visitor to Britain, chiefly as a coastal migrant in early autumn.

 Arboreal insects.

 Nest is situated on the ground in loose undergrowth.

TRACK N° 50

Both song types, the rolling trill and simple series of piping notes, can be heard on the CD.

TRACK N° 51

Song, which is almost like a cross between a Willow Warbler and a Wren, and a series of wagtail-like calls.

52 | Blackcap
Sylvia atricapilla

The Blackcap is a short-distance migrant – birds that nest in northern and eastern Europe tend to spend the winter months in Iberia and Italy. Traditionally it was considered as a summer visitor to Britain, but increasingly birds from eastern Europe have begun to migrate west to winter in Britain. This could be due to milder winters or a proliferation of garden feeding.

The male is plain grey-brown above and paler greyish below, with a jet-black cap. The female is slightly browner above and more buff below, and has a chestnut cap. The species is found in mixed deciduous woodlands, and also in parks and large gardens with dense undergrowth. Their loud, rich warbling song attracts attention, but the birds are often difficult to see in the leafy canopy.

In summer mostly insects, and in autumn and winter these are supplemented by berries and soft fruits.

Builds a tightly woven cup of sedges and grass in brambles, thick bushes or ivy.

TRACK N° 52

The rich warbling song is a beautiful warble lasting a few seconds. Followed by examples of the typical tack call.

53 | Garden Warbler
Sylvia borin

The Garden Warbler is one of our most nondescript birds, being entirely grey-buff with no notable distinguishing features. It is also a genuine skulker, so is more often heard than seen. It breeds in rich broadleaved and mixed woodlands, and sometimes also in parks and large gardens with patches of dense undergrowth. It is a summer visitor to Britain and most other parts of Europe, and spends the winter in tropical Africa.

 Mostly insects but also feasts on berries in late summer and autumn to build up its reserves prior to migration.

 Close to ground in a tangle of brambles, nettles or other dense vegetation.

54 | Spotted Flycatcher
Muscicapa striata

The Spotted Flycatcher is a rather plain, dull grey-brown above and whitish below, with profuse brown streaking on the breast. It is most often seen swooping from a perch to pursue and catch flying insects. It has broad mandibles to facilitate catching prey in this way. Common in open woodland of all types, including parks and gardens, it is a summer visitor to most parts of Europe and winters in Africa. Its population is declining in Britain.

 Flying insects, taken on the wing.

 A scruffy nest of grass and moss in a sheltered cavity in a tree, wall, ivy or a building.

TRACK N° 53

Warbling song, which is rather similar to that of the Blackcap but contains less fluty notes. Also the irritable *chek-chek* call.

 TRACK N° 54

Simple song followed by warning calls near the nest and finally 'normal' calls.

55 | Robin
Erithacus rubecula

With its red-orange breast and confiding ways, the Robin is one of our most familiar and popular birds. Found throughout Europe, it is mainly resident, but migrates south and west from colder regions in the winter.

The plumage is brown above and whitish on the belly, with red covering the entire face and breast and bordered by grey. In stature the species often appears plump and neck-less, with spindly legs and frequently with drooping wings. The sexes are alike, but the juveniles often confuse the inexperienced observer as they are entirely brown, with spots and scaling over their whole body.

Worms and small insects. Often forages on the ground. Takes seeds, berries and fruits in autumn and winter.

Scruffy structure of dead leaves and grass built in a hedge, hole in a wall and occasionally in sheds, old kettles and even cast-off shoes!

TRACK N° 55

First the song, heard most of the year except in the post-breeding season. It is more eager in spring, but somewhat melancholic in autumn and winter. Song followed by tick calls.

56 | Thrush Nightingale
Luscinia luscinia

In Europe, this is the northern and eastern counterpart of the Nightingale. It breeds from Denmark and Sweden eastwards, but is a very rare visitor to Britain. It winters in Africa. Like the Nightingale, it is a splendid songster.

In appearance it is very like the Nightingale, but not so red-brown overall: the upperparts are a darker shade of brown and the upperside of the tail especially is not so rich chestnut. The breast is mottled brown-grey, but this feature can be very hard to see in the field, and there is usually a hint of a 'moustache' pattern.

Habitat preference is also similar to that of the Nightingale, but often with a damper element, and it has a liking for swamp forest and stream-side vegetation. Like its close relative, it can often be very skulking and the song, which can carry for miles on a still spring evening, is often the best clue to its presence. It sings both day and night.

Predominantly invertebrates such as worms and insects, while in autumn berries and fruits make up a greater proportion of the diet.

A cup of grasses and other vegetation located in dense, shady shrubbery.

57 | Nightingale
Luscinia megarhynchos

The Nightingale is justly famous for its song, which has immortalized it in literature and folklore. However, the bird itself has reclusive habits and a fairly plain plumage that is red-brown above and grey and buff below, enlivened only by a rich chestnut-coloured tail.

It is a summer visitor with a range that is widespread across southern and western Europe. In Britain it is found only in southern and central parts of England.

The species inhabits woodlands and mature scrub with a good layer of undergrowth, and it is sometimes found in parks and large gardens. It is an inveterate skulker in thick cover, and were it not for the loud, varied song, which can be delivered either during the day or night, it could be easily overlooked.

 Invertebrates such as worms and insects, with berries and fruit taken in late summer and autumn prior to migration.

 Built of dead leaves and grass in thick cover on or near the ground.

TRACK N° 57

Song loud and rich, perhaps more varied in tempo than Thrush Nightingale and containing more series of whistled piping notes. Song followed by high-pitched *iihp* calls.

58 | Pied Flycatcher
Ficedula hypoleuca

The male is very distinctive, being black above with bold white wing-patches. Females and immatures have brown upperparts with much-reduced wing-patches. In all plumages the underparts are plain white. It is most frequently seen as it sallies from a perch for flying insects. It breeds over much of northern and central Europe, and favours mixed and deciduous woodlands, especially oak woods, but also nests in parks and large gardens. In Britain its breeding strongholds are in the north and west; it is a scarce passage visitor elsewhere. It spends the winter in West Africa.

 Mostly flying insects, which are taken on the wing.

 A hole in a mature tree, and takes readily to nestboxes.

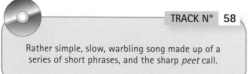

TRACK N° **58**

Rather simple, slow, warbling song made up of a series of short phrases, and the sharp *peet* call.

59 | Red-breasted Flycatcher
Ficedula parva

A bird of tall deciduous and mixed forests in Eastern Europe, from where it migrates south-east in autumn, it is a scarce migrant to Britain and the rest of Western Europe. It is very small, with a plain brown back and white underparts. The adult male sports a blue-grey head and orange-red chin and upper-breast, while both sexes have black tails with bold white patches at the base. These are very obvious when the bird is seen perched with wings typically drooped.

 Arboreal and flying insects.

A cup of moss in the hole of a tree or wall. Takes to nestboxes.

TRACK N° **59**

Song, then two samples of rattling call, reminiscent of Wren, and finally soft whistling call.

60 | Common Redstart
Phoenicurus phoenicurus

The male has stunning plumage. It is grey above, with an orange-red breast, black throat, white forehead and rusty-red tail that is constantly vibrated. The female, by contrast, is drab brown above and whitish-buff below, sometimes tinged rust on the breast, but still has the rusty-red tail. In autumn many young birds resemble the adult female, while males of all ages are subdued in colour due to the pale edges of their freshly moulted plumage.

A true tree-dweller, it is rarely seen on the ground. It breeds across much of Europe and spends the winter in Africa. It is widespread in Britain but absent as a breeding bird from much of south-east England. It breeds in open woodland, including deciduous, coniferous and mixed, and also on heaths with scattered trees and in wooded parks and large gardens.

 Insects and larvae, and more frequently fruit and berries in late summer and autumn. Often feeds like a flycatcher, making aerial sallies after insects.

Nests in a natural hole in a tree, or alternatively will use a hole in a stone wall. Also readily uses nestboxes.

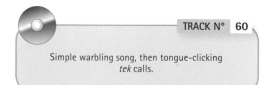

TRACK N° 60

Simple warbling song, then tongue-clicking *tek* calls.

61 | Blackbird
Turdus merula

Common throughout most of Europe, the Blackbird is a familiar species of town parks and gardens, but it is also found in all types of woodland and scrub. It is a very common resident in Britain, with numbers increasing in autumn and winter due to influxes of migrants from colder regions.

The male is all black with an orange-yellow bill, while the female is sooty brown with mottling on the underparts and a paler throat. It has a superb song, which is often delivered from a conspicuous perch from February through to late July.

 Worms, snails, insects, berries and soft fruits including fallen apples.

 Constructs a lined grass cup, usually in a hedge or bush.

TRACK N° 61

Beautiful fluty song, then the *sree* call.

62 | Fieldfare
Turdus pilaris

This large, attractive thrush is a common breeding bird in much of northern and eastern Europe. It migrates south and west for the winter and is predominately a common winter visitor to Britain.

It has a grey head and rump, reddish-brown back and black tail. The breast is yellowish, tinged with heavy dark spotting on a white belly. In flight, it shows a whitish underwing like Mistle Thrush. It breeds in birches and pines, even in town parks and gardens, but in winter it can be found in fields and hedgerows in flocks, often in the company of other thrush species.

 Invertebrates including worms and slugs. In autumn and winter berries and fruits, especially fallen apples.

 Well-lined grass cup in a tree. Often in loose colonies,

TRACK N° 62

Two samples of the song, which essentially are repetitive versions of the chattering calls.

63 | Song Thrush
Turdus philomelos

The Song Thrush is a familiar bird of woodlands, forests, parks and gardens, although it is more secretive than the Blackbird. It is a common bird throughout most of Europe. The resident population in Britain is supplemented in winter by migrants from more northern and eastern breeding populations, which come here to take advantage of our milder winters. In all plumages, birds are plain brown above and white with heavy dark-brown spotting below. In flight, it shows orange-buff patches on the underwings.

Song Thrushes breed in most types of woodland, and also in parks and gardens. They begin to sing as early as December, and have a beautiful strong song of whistling and liquid notes, rather similar to the song of the Blackbird, but they repeat each phrase, sometimes several times. A male may have a repertoire of more than a hundred phrases, copied from neighbouring birds and its parents. The song may also include mimicry of man-made objects such as telephones.

 Invertebrates such as worms, snails and insects, with seeds, berries and fruits in autumn and winter. Snails are extracted by hammering the shells on a stone known as an 'anvil'.

A bowl of moss and grass lined with mud and located in a tree, ivy or hedge.

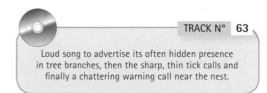

TRACK N° 63

Loud song to advertise its often hidden presence in tree branches, then the sharp, thin tick calls and finally a chattering warning call near the nest.

51

64 | Redwing
Turdus iliacus

Similar in plumage and size to the Song Thrush, the Redwing has rusty-red on the flanks and a prominent white supercilium that can be picked out at distance. The underwings and flanks are a bold rusty-red.

Redwings are very common breeders in the conifer and birch forests of northern Europe. They migrate south and west in autumn, and they are common winter visitors to Britain, where they often join roving flocks of thrushes and are seen in the company of Fieldfares. They are nocturnal migrants and the soft *tsee* call is a characteristic sound of autumn nights in Western Europe.

 Worms, ground-dwelling insects, berries.

 In a bush, tree or stump. A rare breeder in Britain.

65 | Mistle Thrush
Turdus viscivorus

Conspicuously larger than the Song Thrush, the Mistle Thrush is much more grey-brown above, emphasized by pale fringes to the wing feathers, giving it an overall paler appearance. In flight the underwing shows white. It is mostly resident in Western Europe, but northern and eastern breeders are more migratory. It breeds in woods, parks and large gardens, often in semi-urban areas, but It tends to be more of a bird of open fields in winter.

 Berries and fruits, worms, snails and slugs.

 A large, conspicuous grass bowl often in the fork of a tall tree.

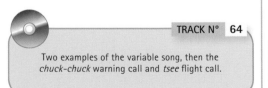

TRACK N° **64**

Two examples of the variable song, then the *chuck-chuck* warning call and *tsee* flight call.

TRACK N° **65**

First the song, which sounds like a more solemn version of the Blackbird's, followed by typical dry, rattling calls.

66 | Dunnock
Prunella modularis

This unobtrusive sparrow-sized bird has brown-streaked upperparts with a lavender-grey head, breast and belly. It is most often seen as it creeps jerkily and mouse-like on the ground, but it quickly moves into low cover if disturbed.

In Britain and much of Western Europe, it is a common resident of gardens and parks (even in urban areas), farmland with hedgerows, and woodland edges and clearings. In northern Europe, where migratory, it is a bird of dense forest, especially spruce plantations.

 Insects and other small invertebrates, and seeds.

 Constructs a foundation of twigs on which a cup of grass and moss is built, in a hedge or thick bush.

67 | Tree Pipit
Anthus campestris

The Tree Pipit is a typical pipit, being brown with dark streaking above and buff-white below, and strongly marked on the breast but less so on the flanks. It breeds across Europe in open woodland, also on heaths and commons with plenty of trees, and winters in Africa. It is easiest to see while performing song flights in spring, when it flies up from a favoured perch in a tree and 'parachutes' slowly back down again, singing throughout. If often 'pumps' its tail downwards when perched.

 Insects and occasionally seeds.

 Builds a nest of grasses concealed in a tussock or bank on the ground and seldom far from trees.

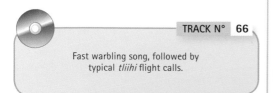

68 | Waxwing
Bombycilla garrulus

The Waxwing breeds in Europe's northernmost coniferous forests, but in winter migrates south and reaches Britain in varying numbers each year. So-called 'invasion' years occur when the Scandinavian berry crop fails and the birds disperse across Western Europe. Waxwings are starling-sized with an unmistakable large, erect crest. The upperparts are brownish and grey, while the head, breast and belly have a pinkish hue. They have a black chin and mask through the eye, while the flight feathers and tail tip are edged yellow. Small, waxy, red patches on the wings of the adults give the species its name.

 Insects in spring and summer, berries and hips in autumn and winter.

 Usually high up in a pine in older forests.

 TRACK N° **68**

Distinctive silvery, trilling calls by a flock.

69 | Rustic Bunting
Emberiza rustica

The Rustic Bunting is a summer visitor to swampy coniferous and mixed forests in northern Europe. It migrates south-eastwards in autumn to spend the winter in South-East Asia, so it is rare elsewhere in Europe and is a rare migrant to Britain, mainly in spring and autumn. It is the size of a Reed Bunting, only with streaked brown upperparts, white below, red-brown streaking on the flanks, a red-brown 'shawl' and breast-band. Its head is boldly patterned black and white. Females are similar to males, but more with more subdued colours, and the black on the head of the male is replaced by brown.

 Mainly seeds, although takes predominantly insects in the breeding season.

 On the ground, often in tussock grass and frequently near water.

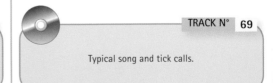 TRACK N° **69**

Typical song and tick calls.

70 | Chaffinch
Fringilla coelebs

One of Europe's commonest birds, the Chaffinch is found in all types of woodland, as well as in parks and gardens. It is resident in Britain, but in winter numbers are swelled by the arrival of bird migrants, which bred in colder climes. It often forms winter flocks with other species of finch.

The male Chaffinch is a handsome, colourful bird with pinkish-red on the cheeks and breast, and a blue-grey crown and nape. In the female the bright colours are replaced by more subdued browns, buffs and greys. Both sexes are brownish and blackish above, with two bold white wing-bars, and show a prominent greenish rump in flight.

The Chaffinch's song is powerful, and males typically sing two or three different song types.

 Mainly insects in summer, seeds at other times. Visits bird feeders.

Builds a superbly woven cup of moss and lichens bound with spiders' webs, usually in the fork of a tree or in a hedge or bush. The female incubates the eggs and the young are fed by both parents.

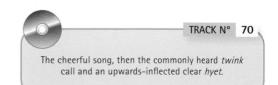

TRACK N° 70

The cheerful song, then the commonly heard *twink* call and an upwards-inflected clear *hyet*.

71 | Brambling
Fringilla montifringilla

The Brambling is a winter visitor to much of Europe, including Britain, where it often joins flocks of other finches, sometimes in great numbers where there has been a good fall of beechmast. It breeds in alpine birch forests from Fenno-Scandinavia eastwards.

The breeding male is black above and orange below, with a white belly and vent, but this plumage is only seen in Western Europe in late spring. At other times the male resembles the female, with the head and back brownish and grey and with less orange on the breast. In flight it shows a prominent white rump in all plumages.

 Beechmast, hornbeam nuts, seeds and berries. Will visit feeders.

 In fork of a birch tree.

72 | Pine Grosbeak
Pinicola enucleator

The male is carmine-red with darker wings and tail, the female greyish and yellow. A large finch, as big as a Starling, it is long-tailed and bull-necked. It breeds in Europe's taiga region in undisturbed coniferous forest with bilberry and crowberry, where it is very difficult to locate in the breeding season. However, at other times of year they are not shy and are regular visitors to bird feeders. It erupts south in numbers during years of food scarcity. It is a very rare vagrant to Britain.

 Seeds, berries, buds and shoots.

 A platform of twigs and moss, usually in a spruce.

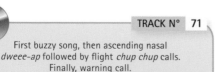

TRACK N° 71

First buzzy song, then ascending nasal *dweee-ap* followed by flight *chup chup* calls. Finally, warning call.

TRACK N° 72

Song, calls and subsong consisting of a series of various calls.

73 | Greenfinch
Chloris chloris

As the name suggests, this finch is more or less green all over, but with yellow fringes to the wings and tail. The male is bright yellow-green in spring and summer, while the male in winter and the female are more grey-green with less yellow. Juveniles are paler, greyer and more streaky overall. It has a stout bill that turns pink on the breeding male.

The Greenfinch is mainly resident and common over most of Europe, including Britain. It breeds on the edge of woodlands and forests, and in copses, parks and gardens. In winter it also inhabits more open country, especially farmland.

The Greenfinch is resident everywhere in Britain. The birds often perch on the tops of trees and bushes, attracting attention with their persistent nasal calls.

 Mainly seeds, berries and buds, but in summer feeds the young mainly on insects. A regular visitor to bird feeders.

A loose structure of twigs and grass lined with moss in a bush, tree or an overgrown hedge – often favours small conifers and evergreen bushes.

TRACK N° 73

First a simple song consisting of simple buzzing elements, then more complex song with warbling and trilling elements.

74 | Parrot Crossbill
Loxia pytyopsittacus

In all plumages the Parrot Crossbill is very similar in appearance to the Common Crossbill – red male, green-and-grey female and streaked juvenile – but has an even bigger head and a heavier, more evenly thick bill. A pine specialist in Europe, it is confined to Fenno-Scandinavia and is rarely seen elsewhere other than during infrequent irruptions south when the pine crop fails. It is a rare visitor to Britain but has bred in the past.

 Conifer seeds, mainly of pine and spruce. Insects also during the breeding season.

 High in a conifer, often at the forest edge.

75 | Common Crossbill
Loxia curvirostra

Breeding in Europe's coniferous forest, including those in Britain, it has a patchy distribution, being common in some areas and absent from others. It is largely dependent on spruce seeds, and when this crop fails they migrate and 'invade' areas where food is more plentiful. It has a disproportionately large head and a bill with the mandibles crossed at the tip to enable the extraction of seeds from spruce cones. The male is reddish with darker wings, the female grey-green and streaked darker, with a yellowish-green rump.

 Conifer seeds, especially spruce, with some berries and insects.

 Nests as early as February to coincide with opening of spruce cones; builds a cup on a platform of twigs on the branch of a conifer.

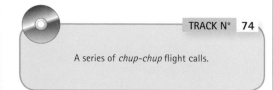

TRACK N° **74**

A series of *chup-chup* flight calls.

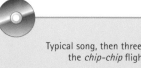

TRACK N° **75**

Typical song, then three samples of the *chip-chip* flight call.

76 | Lesser Redpoll
Carduelis cabaret

The Lesser Redpoll is smaller than the Chaffinch and is a rather nondescript grey-and-brown-streaked finch, but it has a bright red fore-crown or 'poll' and a small black bib. The belly and undertail-coverts are white. The breast is buffish and streaked at the sides, and when breeding the breast of the male becomes variably suffused pinkish-red. Juveniles lack the red poll and have less black on the chin than the adults.

In winter, our resident Lesser Redpolls are joined by migratory Common Redpolls *Carduelis flammea* from northern Europe. These birds are superficially similar to Lesser Redpolls, but they are larger and paler. The species is a birch zone specialist, but also breeds in young conifers, spruce and even open areas with bushes. The songs and calls of Lesser and Common Redpolls are extremely similar.

 Seeds, especially those of birch, alder and grasses, and also fruit buds and invertebrates.

 A small cup of grass and moss high in a bush or tree. The nest is built by the female, and she incubates the eggs while being fed by the male.

TRACK N° 76

First the song, which consists of a series of long, rolling buzzing notes, then slowly repeated *chechechecheche* calls.

77 | Goldfinch
Carduelis carduelis

This beautiful finch was once much prized as a cagebird. It has a bright red face, with rest of head black and white. The body is tawny-brown above, while the underparts are paler. The black wings have bold golden-yellow wing-bars and white spots. It is adept at extracting seeds from thistle heads and is often found feeding on these in autumn and winter. It is a common resident of woodlands, copses and gardens thoughout most of Europe.

 Mainly seeds of trees, thistles and teasels. Also takes insects in summer. Increasingly visits bird feeders.

 Builds a neat cup filled with moss, lichens and thistledown in a tree, large bush or dense hedges.

78 | Siskin
Carduelis spinus

The Siskin is a small greenish finch, streaked darker above, with a yellow rump and wing-bars and a white belly. The male has a yellow breast and a black cap and chin. The female and juvenile are more heavily streaked. It has a very sharply pointed bill to extract conifer seeds from half-open pine or spruce cones. It is common in conifers and mixed forest with southward and westward movement in winter, especially to Britain.

 Seeds of pine and spruce, but mainly alder in winter. Can be attracted to bird feeders.

 A nest constructed of fir twigs high in a conifer or spruce.

TRACK N° 77
A vocal bird with a variety of calls. Here a bright, fast, tinkling, rattling and trilling song, which is quite complex and usually recognizable by the inclusion of some *twiddit* call notes.

TRACK N° 78
First the song, a rapid, undulating trilling, twittering and repeated call notes. Then some downwards-inflected clear *dju'ii* calls.

79 | Bullfinch
Pyrrhula pyrrhula

This is a large handsome finch that looks bull-necked. The male is bright pinkish-red below and blue-grey above, with a black cap and dark wings with a bold white wing-bar. The female is similarly patterned, but greyish-brown above and greyish-buff below. Unobtrusive in habits, the white rump in flight is often the best clue to identity when views are brief. It is a resident found over most of Europe, including Britain, inhabiting woodland, large gardens and orchards. Birds in Northern Europe are larger, brighter, and frequent dense forest.

 Seeds and berries in autumn and winter, buds and insects in spring and summer.

 A platform of twigs in a bush or low tree.

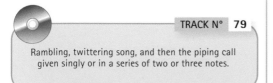

TRACK N° 79

Rambling, twittering song, and then the piping call given singly or in a series of two or three notes.

80 | Hawfinch
Coccothraustes coccothraustes

This large finch has a bull-neck and a massive conical bill to crack kernels. It is reddish-brown above, paler below, becoming greyish-white on the lower belly and undertail. It has a grey nape, black chin and large white patch on the shoulder of the dark wings. Very unobtrusive, it is seldom seen in its preferred habitats of deciduous and mixed woods, parks and large gardens. In winter it forms small flocks and occasionally visits feeders. It is found in suitable habitat in most of Europe, including Britain, where it tends to be rare and retiring in nature.

 Kernels, seeds, berries and insects.

 High in a tree, often on a horizontal bough.

TRACK N° 80

First simple song, then *zseeh* calls.

Other Natural History Books by New Holland Publishers

Advanced Bird ID Handbook:
The Western Palearctic
Nils van Duivendijk. Award-winning and innovative field guide covering the key features of every important plumage of all 1,350 species and subspecies that have ever occurred in Britain, Europe, North Africa and the Middle East. Published in association with the journal *British Birds*. £24.99 ISBN 978 1 78009 022 1.
Also available: **Advanced Bird ID Guide:**
The Western Palearctic £14.99 ISBN 978 1 84773 607 9.

Bill Oddie's Birds of Britain & Ireland
Bill Oddie. A new and fully updated edition of this popular title. Ideal for any birder coming to grips with the 200 or so most common species. Written in Bill's own inimitable style, the book includes all the latest updates, while a unique feature is the 10 pages featuring 'confusion species'. £12.99 ISBN 978 1 78009 245 4

Birds: Magic Moments
Markus Varesvuo. Bringing together the work of one of the world's best bird photographers, this is a celebration of the avian world, illustrating rarely observed scenes from courtship, nest-building, hunting and raising young. The author's stunning images cover species ranging from colourful bee-eaters to majestic eagles. £20 ISBN 978 1 78009 075 7
Also available: **Fascinating Birds** £20, ISBN 978 1 78009 178 5.

New Holland Concise Bird Guide
An ideal first field guide to British birds for children or adults. Includes more than 250 species and 800 colour artworks. Published in association with The Wildlife Trusts. £4.99 ISBN 978 1 84773 601 7.
Other Concise Guides include (all £4.99):
Butterfly and Moth ISBN 978 1 84773 602 4, **Garden Bird** ISBN 978 1 84773 978 0, **Garden Wildlife** ISBN 978 1 84773 606 2, **Herb** ISBN 978 1 84773 976 6, **Insect** ISBN 978 1 84773 604 8, **Mushroom** ISBN 978 1 84773 785 4, **Pond Wildlife** ISBN 978 1 84773 977 3, **Seashore Wildlife** ISBN 978 1 84773 786 1, **Tree** ISBN 978 1 84773 605 5 and **Wild Flower** ISBN 978 1 84773 603 1.

New Holland European Bird Guide
Peter H Barthel. The only truly pocket-sized comprehensive field guide to all the birds of Britain and Europe. Features more than 1,700 beautiful and accurate artworks of more than 500 species. £10.99 ISBN 978 1 84773 110 4.

Peregrine Falcon
Patrick Stirling-Aird. Beautifully illustrated book detailing the life of this remarkable raptor, and offering a window into a rarely seen world. Contains more than 80 stunning colour photographs. £14.99 ISBN 978 1 84773 769 4.
Also available: **Barn Owl** (£14.99, ISBN 978 1 84773 768 7). **Kingfisher** (£12.99, ISBN 978 1 84773 524 9).

See www.newhollandpublishers.com for more than 200 Natural History titles

TRACK LISTING

INDEX

Roman type = English name
Italic type = Latin name